Imagine

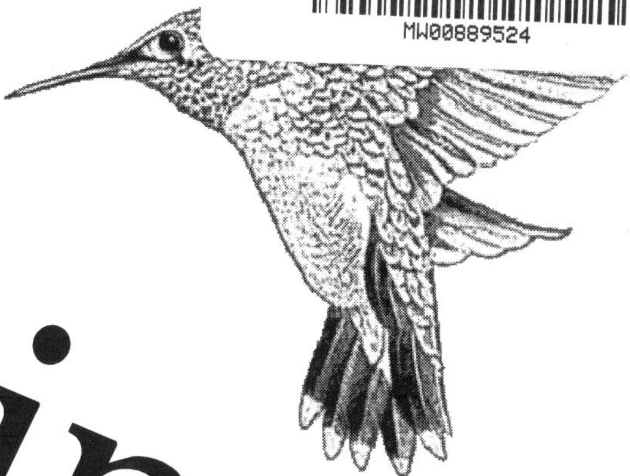

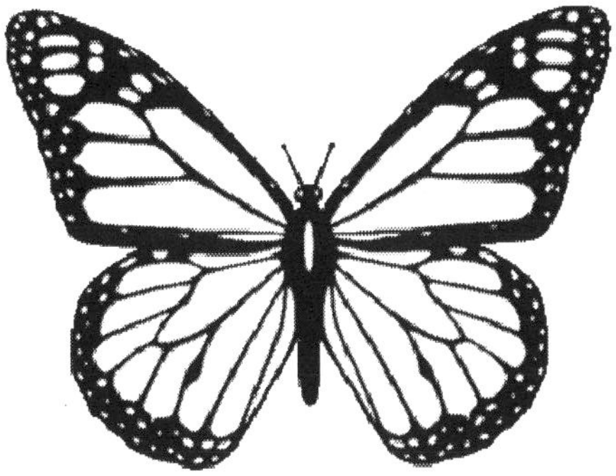

Dream

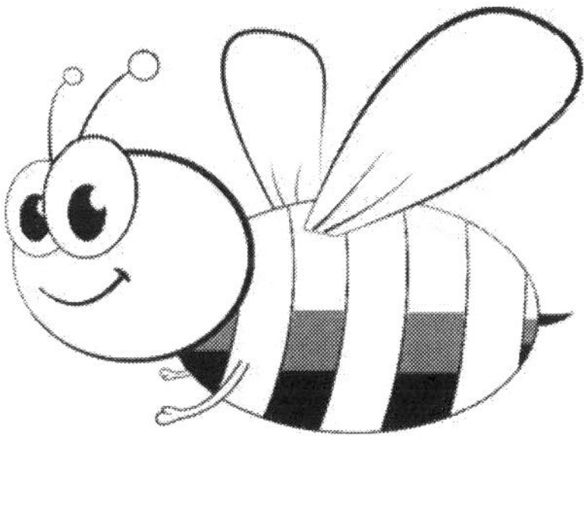

Believe

Snow Canyon Publishing

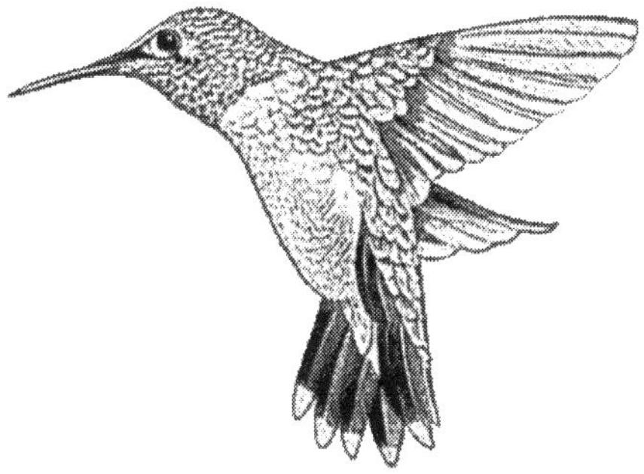

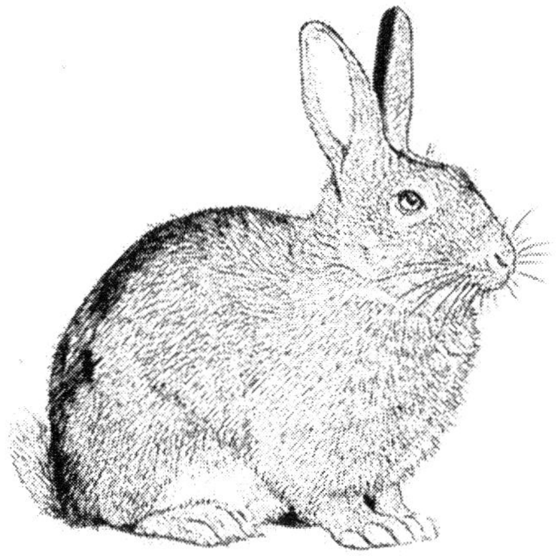

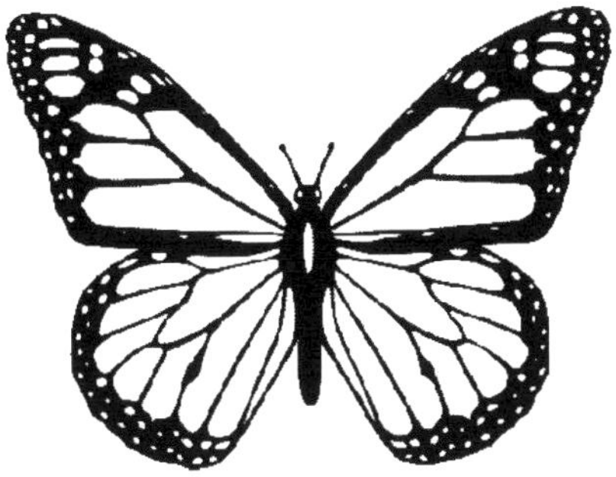

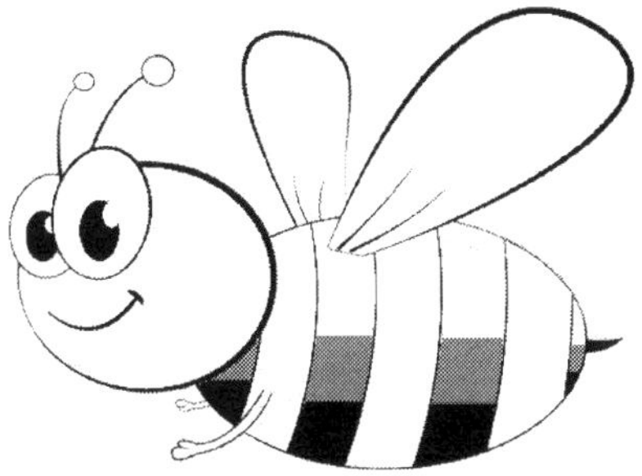

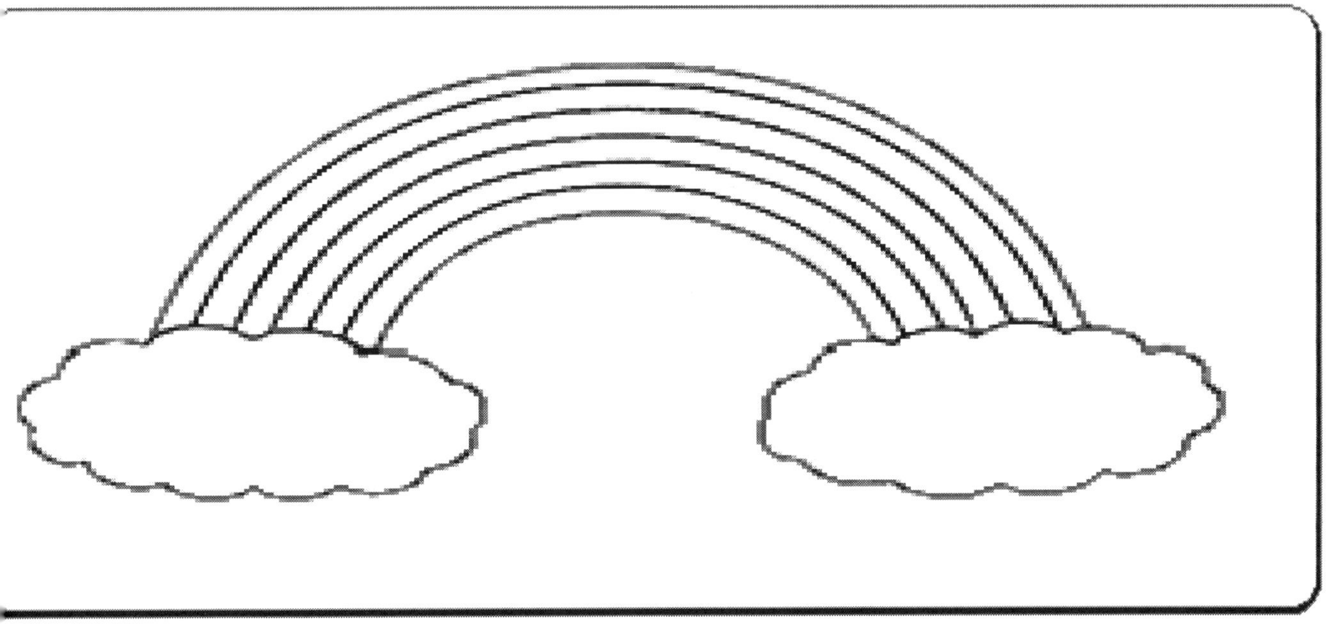

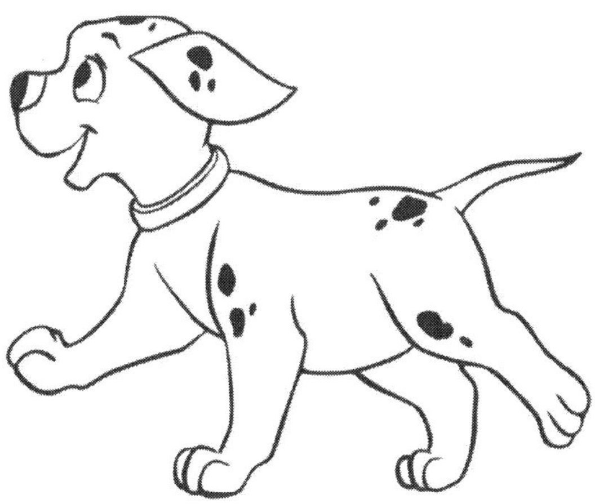

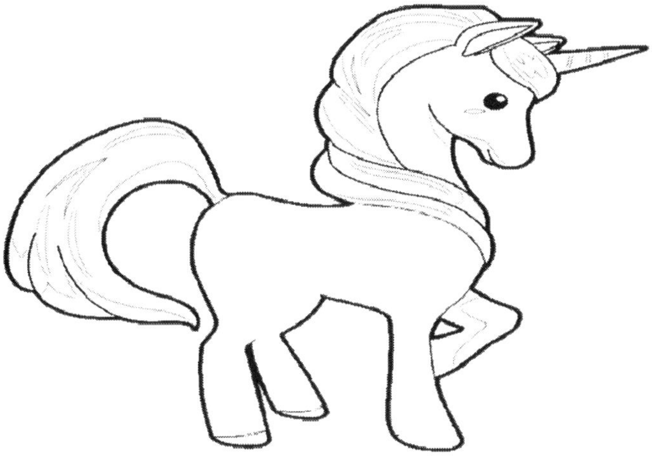

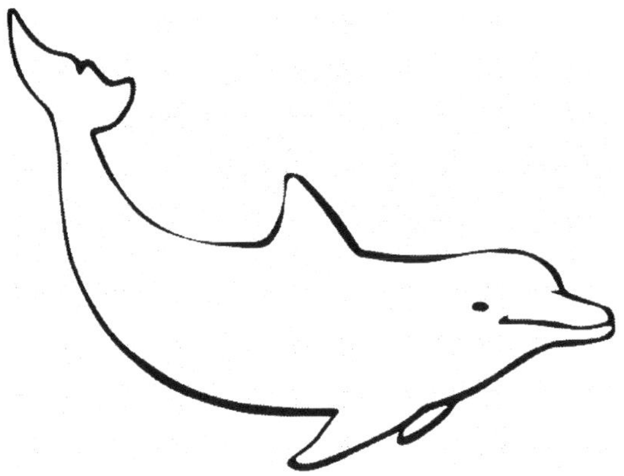

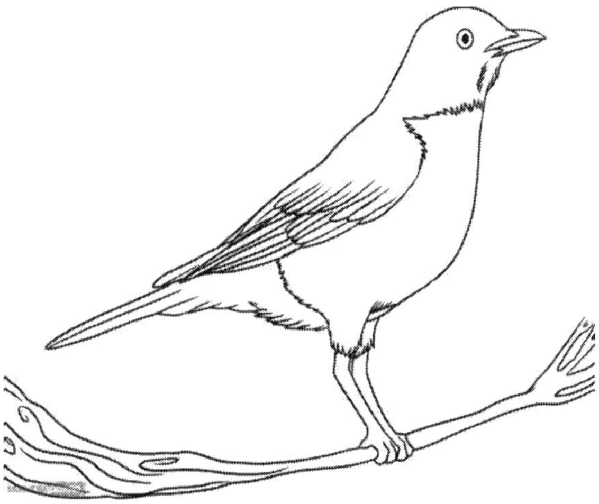

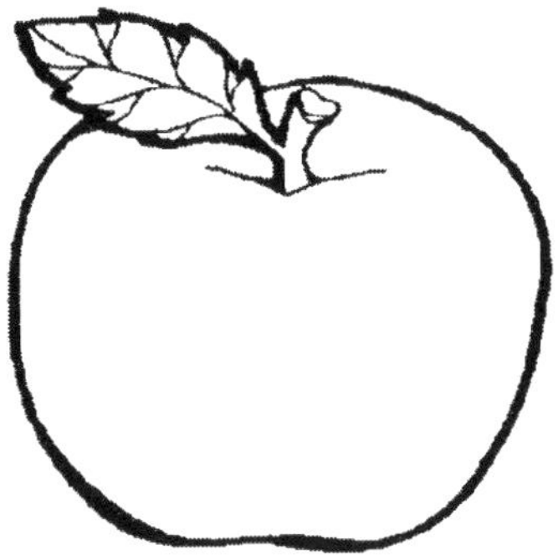

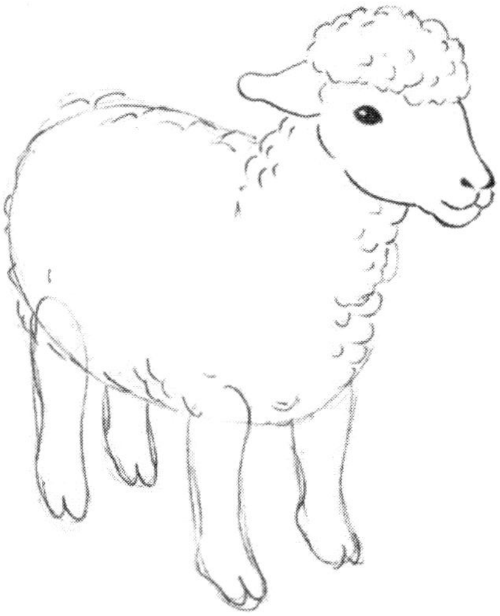

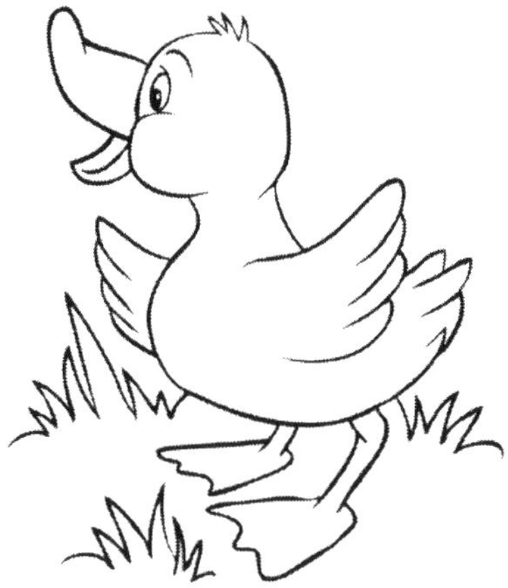

Made in the USA
Middletown, DE
14 September 2020

19853664R00057